A Spark in the Dark

JOYCE B. CARTER

PublishAmerica
Baltimore

At the specific preference of the author, PublishAmerica allowed this work to remain exactly as the author intended, verbatim, without editorial input.

ISBN: 1-4241-1228-1
PUBLISHED BY PUBLISHAMERICA, LLLP
www.publishamerica.com
Baltimore

Printed in the United States of America

Acknowledgments

I would like to acknowledge the people who were there during my darkest times, giving me the encouragement and strength to keep moving forward. Without them, this book would never have been written. To my son Eric Carter and step-daughters Becky and Amber, thank you for your love. To my siblings, Laureen, David, Wanda, and John, your encouragement gave me courage to continue. To Pastors Craig and Sandy Taylor, your example breaths life into those you lead.

A Spark in the Dark

Where there is light, there can be no darkness.

When I was young my family went on a cave tour. As part of the tour the guide turned off the lights so we could fully appreciate the total darkness. God recently brought that experience to mind as I considered writing this book. He pointed out to me that darkness is the absence of light. Had there been one tiny spark in that cave, the darkness would have been totally destroyed.

Portions of our lives are sometimes wrapped in darkness because we do not have a clear understanding of the words we hear and use. My prayer is that examining and explaining some of the most misunderstood words used in the Christian culture will create an explosion of sparks into those areas of darkness, producing a wild fire of light and freedom.

*I*ntroduction

In all circumstances God works on an individual
level with every individual present.

God is a God of detail who concentrates on each on of us
specifically. He is very concerned with every detail of our lives.
His desire is that we live abundant lives, without darkness or
despair.

Unfortunately, the Christian culture is full of words with half
or entirely misunderstood meanings. Those words are often
given definitions in opposition to Biblical definitions because of
our worldly upbringing. People with little or no experience in the
church are frequently confused, or repelled by the exhortation to
be humble, meek or longsuffering because of the stigma placed
on the words outside of the Bible. Others cling to the worldly
definitions, thinking they much be doormats and enablers to
exemplify the characteristics God desires in them.

I grew up in a good, loving family but we rarely entered a
church. My parents believed in God but had not accepted Jesus
as Lord so I was not raised in an environment where the most
common Christian words were used. Since I spent four years in
college during the early feminist movement, I was often exposed

to the worldly definitions and the world's concepts of what the church teaches. When I first accepted Jesus as Lord I began to hear many words used the first time in a Biblical context. They didn't agree with the definitions I had learned outside of church. Everyone seemed to know exactly what they meant so I felt foolish asking. Instead I did what many people do, I developed definitions based upon the word's use in sentences. Frankly, it made many of the words about as clear as mud and opened the door for some real problems and mistakes in my life.

Over time I have discovered I am not unique in this area. Many people not raised in the church, even some who are, did exactly the same thing I did. For some it has created a strangle hold on their lives. For others, it has produced some deep pits that are difficult to climb out of.

This book is designed to define and explain some of the words that are most often misunderstood. Definitions are easily obtained by going to a dictionary but understanding is a different matter. Since many words in the English language can have wildly different meanings we need to dig deeper and compare the words to their uses to gain a clear understanding. Often the complete meaning of a word can not be appreciated until we examine the original Hebrew or Greek since both languages were developed to express concepts through association and mental images.

Developing understanding puts me in mind of a crystal ball a friend of mine had. The outer surface was composed of many flat surfaces. The base was covered with black felt. As you turned the ball, the interior color changed, depending upon how the light was broken. Nothing about the ball changed except your perspective of the interior. Understanding is similar to the crystal ball. As we hold a word to the light of God's wisdom we see more colors and meanings exposed. Like the ball, the word doesn't change but is seen from God's perspective. We begin to discern how He wishes us to apply the meaning in our lives.

To paraphrase Solomon, understanding and wisdom bring

happiness. Completely understanding the definition of a word is seeing it's application to life. Wisdom comes from having the knowledge and understanding. Understanding and wisdom will not give you peace unless it is fed by an infinite source of light. My hope is that understanding will give you the ability to more easily see that source and where it is working in your life.

The Will

I suspect most of us understand the will but perhaps not the exact role it plays in our lives. It is probably the greatest blessing God has given humans, and, can also be, the greatest curse. Use of our will can lead us to a more abundant life than we ever imagined or carry us into the darkest pit.

There are an amazing number of Hebrew words translated as "will". A short list includes:

The seat of our emotions, passions and courage

Our desires

Our consent

Our acceptance

Our heart

The heart of our moral character

The will is what drives our actions and decisions. It is the heart of our being. How we use it determines which choices we make through out our lives. Whatever sits in the driver's seat of your will is directly responsible for your actions and words. Jesus understood this well when He said:

> *What makes a person unclean is not what goes into his mouth, rather what comes out of his mouth, that is what makes him unclean!*
> Matthew 15:11 (Complete Jewish Bible)

In other words, if your will is driven by your selfish desires you will choose actions that separate you from God. If your will is driven by Godly desires you will make decisions that will honor God and draw others to Him.

Your will is always yours. God will never override it or require you be a puppet controlled by some unseen hand. It is always your option to do as God asks and follow God's lead or to say no. Understand as well that choosing not to follow God's leading will not bring down the wrath of God or cause Him to set on His throne calculating your demise. It will sadden Him because you are choosing to separate yourself from Him and His protection as well as open doors for greater problems in your life. He will never stop calling you but He will honor your decisions thereby confirming His love and respect for you.

One thing we tend to forget is that we are not the only people with a will and the freedom to choose. Every individual has the gift of free will. Sometimes the choices others make, especially if they are in a position of authority over us, will effect us despite the choices we make. God is required, by His own promises and design, to give everyone the freedom to choose. When this happens we tend to blame God without recognizing the free will of others is at work. It is then that trusting God is the hardest yet the most important because He will arrange all bad experience to result in some good. Trusting God is a matter of using your free will.

Picture it like this, a large bowl sits on a table filled with water, it's surface totally smooth. Holding your hand over the bowl you allow one drop of water from your finger to hit the surface. The result is a series of perfectly concentric circles radiating from the point the droplet hit the water.

Now, hold your hand over the bowl and let a drop fall from all of your fingers. No longer are there perfect circles. Each drop starts those circles but, because they form in different areas, the tiny waves interact and interfere with each other. Each drop affect the others.

If you were the only living human your decisions would produce perfect concentric circles. Because there are other people all around you, producing droplets of decisions, your circles are affected and changed. The amazing thing is that God can take all those independent circles and produce a pattern of beauty. Even those drops that are larger and cause more interference can be used to enhance the beauty.

forgiveness

We all know forgiveness is the act of pardoning or excusing an offense. Although it seems simple enough to define, forgiveness has very deep implications for the Christian, both spiritually and physically. We understand God forgives our sins but often do not fully grasp the importance of our forgiving others.

Completely understanding forgiveness in my life started in a time I was attempting to dig my way out of a deep depression caused by a double betrayal followed by the death of both my parents. While helping with the sound system at a women's meeting I was given the opportunity to select a cup which contained a small pouch holding a word God wanted me to work on through the coming year. To my great distaste I picked a cup that contained the word "forgiveness." I promptly stuck the paper in a pile on my desk hoping it would vanish into the black hole that sucks up mismatched socks and that extra time we all seem to lose.

Several months later, while looking for something, I came across the paper. All my resentment came boiling back to the surface and I became determined to research forgiveness and be done with it. Within 5 minutes God had shattered the darkness surrounding my understanding and destroyed every precon- ceived idea, conclusion and misunderstanding I had. Forgiveness became that many-faceted prism showering my life with light.

I discovered the Hebrew word nasa (or nacah) which is translated forgive literally means to lift up. God revealed to me that when I forgive offenses He is able to lift me up. Forgiveness is about me, lifting me up and out of my darkness.

One of the greatest stumbling blocks for people is the concept that when we forgive, the person we forgive is no longer accountable for their actions. Nothing could be farther from the truth. When God forgives our sins we still have to face the consequences for our actions. So, too do the people we forgive. By forgiving them you are allowing God to lift you out of the darkness and out of the way so they can face those consequences without causing you more harm.

Another hindrance to forgiveness is the concept that when we forgive we forget and have to treat that person as if nothing happened. After all, when God forgives us He forgets our sin. Actually it works more like this, God forgives us and forgets the pain caused by our separation from Him. He does not keep a tally sheet saying that on these dates you separated yourself from Him. He also does not forget who you are and the tendencies in you to move into certain sins. From the point of His forgiveness He uses the renewed bond to guide you away from those traps. He applies His wisdom to His knowledge of who you are.

Likewise, God expects us to use wisdom when dealing with those we forgive. For small, thoughtless actions we do need to forget when we forgive because the person we forgive may just be having a bad day. For actions that break our trust or are cruel, our forgiveness should lift us out of the emotional pain but forgetting would be a lack of wisdom. Broken trust should be remembered to prevent you from trusting an untrustworthy person, but without the need for vengeance or attacks against that person.

For example, I have forgiven those who betrayed me to the

point I am no longer attached to the emotions the memories once created and I can discuss the incident without venom. I have not forgotten the actions, however which proved to protect me and my son from even more serious problems that arose later. By remembering the signs I was able to stay separated from them when their actions resulted in serious consequences. Those consequences could have fallen upon me and my son had I "forgot" when I forgave and walked back into the situation.

For me the best way to understand forgiveness comes when I consider unforgivness as a pit filled with a clingy, tarry substance. The tar is my emotions attached to the incident and as long as I sit in it, playing with my emotions I will see nothing but tar. It will begin to fill every pore and fiber of my being. When I recognize the emotions and choose to forgive, God will lift me out of the pit. He can then clean the tar off and flush out the pit so I can heal. He won't flush the pit until I choose to be lifted out because His desire is to heal not destroy me along with the pit.

Forgiveness

Joyce Carter 2005

Humble (Humility)

The word humble can create widely different images in people's minds. On one hand they see humble people as weak and ineffective who never stand up for themselves. On the other, humble people are lauded for their lack of arrogance and egocentric behavior. Although these concepts are at odds with each other, we tend to apply the word "humble" to them giving us the illusion they are both correct.

Webster defines humble as marked by meekness or modesty in behavior, attitude or spirit, not arrogant or prideful. The ancient Hebrew word kana (pronounced kaw-nah) means to bend the knee. Being humble, then, is with willingness to bend your knee.

When the first nuclear power plant was built at Nine Mile Point in northern New York, my family took the tour provided at the visitor's center. The tour was designed to explain how the plant worked and why it was a safe form of power. As with all young children I remember little of the actual tour except for a room at the beginning. That room was designed to give you the illusion of standing in space. To my eyes it was so well done I actually felt I was unattached to earth and floating in space. It was a tremendously exciting experience, but it also impressed upon me just how very small I was compared to the vastness of the universe. I clearly recall the realization that no matter how big or important I grew, I would still be tiny compared to that vastness. It was my first lesson in humility.

Being humble merely means you are aware you are not the center of everything but play a small and important part in the scheme of the universal plan. This recognition gives you the ability and the will to bend your knee when the situation requires it, such as when you are under another's authority. Humble people recognize they do not have all the answers and are willing to ask for help or information.

To be humble, however, does not require self-abasement or malleability. You do not have to talk yourself down, you simply give proper credit where it is due, not accepting credit for what you have not done. You do not have to do everything others ask or agree to what everyone else says. Humble people are also people who can say no when necessary.

We need to recognize humble people are not necessarily more spiritual than others. As humans we tend to associate characteristics in groups. As Christians we often connect humble and spiritual. It is important to remember humble people are not necessarily more spirit filled or closer to God. There are many people in the world who live modest, humble lives but do not have a relationship with Jesus. Those who know Jesus and are humble share the same spirit as all other Christians. Recognizing humility as a desirable characteristic without placing the humble on a pedestal helps us keep our focus on God.

The humble person lives life knowing and accepting that not all roads lead to them.

Gentleness

Nothing is so strong as real gentleness

Nothing so gentle as real strength

Frances De Sales

Somehow our understanding of gentleness has become warped to include the concepts of being easily swayed, weak, and inept. We discard the concept of gentleness in our lives, preferring the tough "macho" stereotype for both men and women. Interestingly enough we crave gentleness in others and seek for those who are gentle, while at the same time rejecting it when offered. Perhaps if we understood gentleness better we would be more inclined to recognize and embrace it in ourselves and others.

I particularly like the definition of the Hebrew word rak which means tender, soft of words, no armor. Armor is hard, abrasive, designed to be impenetrable. Someone wearing armor makes harsh, grating sounds when they move. Their touch causes abrasions and injuries to others. Armor sends the message to all who see it, "Do not come near me or you will be hurt." Armor gives the impression of great strength but, since it is an exterior shell, it can not stand or move alone. It is an illusionary strength.

Since gentle people do not have armor there is a lack of harshness. The sounds made by gentle people are soothing and soft. The lack of armor means touch is not painful and causes no injury. Gentleness allow others to approach without fear of rejection, pain, or emotional damage. Since gentleness is generated on the inside it provides constant strength and mobility during interaction with others. We often seek out gentle people when we are going through hard times or hurting because we can trust them not to tear open our wounds or dump salt on them.

Gentle people do not pity, coddle, or look down on those round them. They are not inclined to encourage people to remain in bad circumstances or indulge others' emotions. They do have the ability to help someone see what is wrong without driving their point home with a hammer. They tend to show you where the open doors are and encourage you to take them without trying to shove you through against your will.

Gentleness always brings to mind the image of a shepherd. He does not yell at his sheep, knowing it will more often cause them to react in fear, but speaks to them quietly, encouraging them to follow. If one falls into a hole, the shepherd doesn't berate it but carefully lifts it back to safe ground. He doesn't grab it and yank it back to a good path but softly corrects and touches it to guide it to safety. Those who are new born or weak are gently lifted and carried while he speaks kind words.

As with so much else in our lives, gentleness is a choice. It takes effort and diligence to turn from our ungentle, gruff and abrasive natures to more kind and considerate ones. Over time it becomes easier and more natural, especially when we begin to fully appreciate how desirable gentleness is.

A gentle response deflects fury
but a harsh word makes tempers rise.
Proverbs 15:1 (CJB)

Perhaps the greatest key to developing gentleness in our lives is the desire to do no harm. There will often be times in life when people around us are bruised and bleeding. Although gentleness does not mean the problems are dismissed or reduced to insignificance, it will help bind the injuries without creating new ones. Gentle people know there is no need to cut off the arm if there is a scratch or remove a leg because toe nails need to be clipped.

Meekness

Isn't it interesting that all the characteristics Jesus used to describe Himself have been altered into traits of ineptness and weakness?

Take my yoke upon you, and learn from me, for I am meek and lowly in heart; and ye shall find rest in your souls.
(Matt. 11:29 KJV)

Jesus, obviously, was not weak, inept, malleable or indecisive. He had strength, courage, wisdom and walked in integrity at all times.

Meek is defined by Webster as:

1. Showing patience and humility, gentle
2. Easily imposed upon.

The English language is such a joy. In what other language can one word have two exactly opposite meanings?

It doesn't take a great deal of insight or exploration to realize Jesus would have us follow the definition which most clearly describes Him. He, therefore, would have us be called meek because we display patience, humility and gentleness in our lives.

Meekness restrains the natural tendency to retaliate, display one-up-man-ship, treat others harshly or demand everything for ourselves. The meek consider the effects their actions and words will have on others and try to proceed in a manner that will leave others undamaged. This does not mean they will overlook their own needs, both physical and spiritual, only doing things for others. It merely means they will recognize when their actions will hinder or injure others and select a path that comes closest to benefiting all. If that means waiting for someone else it is done without fidgeting or constant reminders of the fact they are waiting.

Being meek does not mean you never express yourself, or only echo what others say. Nor does it mean you only say what you believe others want to hear. When the meek express an opinion it is done with thoughtfulness using words designed to openly and honestly express their thoughts and ideas without force or hints of contempt or sarcasm. They know where they stand and accept that others may not agree. They simply say what they mean and allow others to decide for themselves if they agree or not. Since humility is ingrained in the meek they are willing to work with others, not override them or retreat from them. The meek person has no problems telling someone when they are wrong or their actions will be harmful. They have the ability to say those things without condemnation or attack. They can often tell others things no one else can because they display safe and secure behavior patterns. Others know the meek are not out to control or manipulate them.

The meek are more interested in building. They prefer to see people develop their strengths and create a network of cooperation. They recognize the teamwork of a group does not exist if opinions are not expressed and others' ideas are not considered. They understand that each person is a unique combination of traits and characteristics which improve the success of the group. They also realize that being malleable and changing to suit those around them will lead to disaster. When necessary the meek person can stand firm, however they have the enviable talent of doing so without attacking others or creating chaos.

Mercy

I had a conversation with my nephew recently that emphasized how misunderstood mercy it.[15]He had been informed he was gifted with mercy but was convinced there was no mercy in him. When I told him he didn't understand what mercy was he paused for a moment then asked me to explain. By the time I was done I had the great honor of seeing a lightening in his spirit and the smile that went with, "Yeah, I do that." It's a great joy and blessing to see people fully understand what God has designed in them and how it works.

Mercy is not about "fixing it" . Nor do mercy people coddle those around them. To show mercy does not mean your going to "make it all better." Mercy is not about ignoring consequences, making bad things go away, or telling people there is nothing wrong with them, especially if it is obvious they are dealing with serious problems. It is not about enabling people to remain on destructive paths while patting their emotions so they feel better.

The Hebrew word chacad (pronounced kheh-sed) is translated as mercy. It is derived from the word chacad (khaw-sad) which means to bow the neck. The implication being to choose to look down with favor, compassion and kindness. Mercy is the intellectual choice to show compassion and kindness where judgment is due. When mercy is displayed there is a recognition of the problem, an understanding of it's magnitude, and a lack of demand for payment in full. Without mercy people would be crushed under the weight of their mistakes rather than encouraged to learn from them and move into a life filled with abundance.

Mercy comes in to play most often when some sin is revealed to us. Because we were unaware of it's nature we were unable to deal with it or understand why we were having problems related to it. When God, in His faithfulness, removes the darkness so we can see it clearly, mercy steps in. Revelations of this kind always ignite our feelings, especially those of pain, worthlessness and fear. Without mercy those feelings would rapidly overwhelm us and eventually lead to our death, physically and/or spiritually.

Mercy is the act of sparing us crushing defeat from the emotional baggage of condemnation and judgment without removing the consequences. Yet, at the same time, offering hope and encouragement. Mercy sheds light into dark situations so we can find the road to restoration.

The dynamics work along these lines. We do something or God reveals something to us which sets off the emotional reactions within us. Mercy comes along, from God or through an individual He sends. Mercy says," Yes, you did it, it was wrong, there is great pain here. Your not imagining it. It's real." Instead of demanding the full payment for your actions or patting you on the shoulder and letting you remain where you are, mercy encourages action. "Let's look at how you got here, what traps you fell into and what caused you to take this action." Mercy then seeks to develop a plan to help you deal with the situation, the emotions it created and opens your eyes to the signals that could lead to a repeat. By gently leading someone to discover what happened, mercy reveals the beginning of a path that will get them through the consequences with hope. Notice, mercy does not seek to remove the consequences, merely direct others toward a way to benefit from the situation.

If you have mercy you know that the long range benefits of walking through the consequences far exceed the immediate benefits of removing them. It is true mercy to allow someone the opportunity to learn wisdom, responsibility, develop a good character and learn to trust God because He will not destroy you for mistakes. It is great mercy to assist others to develop the self-esteem to face life knowing there will be help when needed and encouragement to continue.

Mercy people know it is not easy to face consequences so they will continue to offer encouragement and support through the process. They will be there to help them see when there has been progress. They will offer support and help to keep them from being overwhelmed or depressed. They will not, however, pick it up for them.

Mercy also has a similar role in the lives of people who find themselves in bad circumstances through no fault of their own. Because free will applies to everyone we sometimes are faced with consequences created by another person's actions. The application of mercy here is the same. Assistance is offered if needed immediately to provide food, shelter, or clothing but the greatest mercy comes from helping them develop a plan of action without condemning them for trusting the untrustworthy or believing a lie.

In every case mercy fully understands that the ultimate success or failure on the paths a person walks is determined by that person. When you offer mercy it is important to remember you can not do it for them. Your part is to listen, encourage, offer hope, offer direction and help them learn or relearn what they need to succeed. This is the most vulnerable part of mercy and requires the greatest strength.

Compassion

The greatest difference between mercy and compassion is the emotional side. Mercy knows and understands emotions but tends to work on a more intellectual level since mercy chooses aid over judgment. Compassion connects to the emotions. Compassion is the ability to understand and emphasize with others emotions and includes a desire to do something about it. The greatest gift of compassion is helping people connect to others, removing the sense of isolation. It is incredibly easy for humans to feel isolated and alone because we are mentally isolated from the rest of humanity. We hear only our own thoughts and feel only our own emotions, producing the illusion that we are alone among many and that our feelings are unique to us. Compassion is capable of communicating to others their feelings are not unique. Compassion can help bring about a sense of belonging to those around us, they are part of a community and cared for.

Healthy compassion arises from our own circumstances, problems and experiences. We know the feelings others are expressing because we have been there or have been exposed to similar experiences. The details may vary but the pain of loss, frustration from unfair and insensitive people or the fear of financial lack can be shared by anyone who has been there.

Acknowledging their feelings as real and expressing understanding is the compassion that lifts isolation.

That is not to say that compassion encourages others to remain in whatever situation they are in. Nor does it mean they chant "Oh you poor thing." To do either changes compassion to pity. Pity comes from an elevated, arrogant platform while compassion retains the connection and understanding associated with their experiences.

Compassion also, like mercy, is not going to "fix it" for people. Like mercy people, people of compassion will not coddle others. Although they often see things they can do to help and are willing to help, compassionate people do not pick up other's burdens as their own. They are there when someone needs to talk, offer insights from their own experiences and keep communication open with others. They will sit with you through grief without giving "pep talks" to get you moving or ridicule you for your grief. They understand people need time to deal with their feelings. The greatest message compassion sends is, "You are not alone."

Compassion walks hand in hand with mercy and arm in arm with gentleness. For some, compassion may be the only God-light they can see and understand.

Coddling

It seems important to say a few words about coddling. Many who desire to show mercy and compassion step over the line into the area of coddling without recognizing it. Others think it is necessary to coddle to express mercy or compassion. Coddling is very dangerous and can damage those we are trying to help. It is extremely important to refrain from coddling those who are injured. It inhibits growth and often creates resentment.

When we coddle we are babying them. We are treating them as infants, implying they are incapable of growth and maturity. If you are coddling others you are consigning them to a life of dependency and stunted spirituality. They become dependent upon you rather than God and, because God wants them to grow while the coddler keeps them from growing, there will eventually be a rift either between you or between them and God. This can result in resentment because God designed us to grow and we will eventually be irritated by someone's attempts to baby us.

Another way to look at coddling is more visual. To coddle can mean to cook in water just below the boiling point. The idea being that by keeping the water temperature below boiling there are no disturbances in the water (bubbles) and the food will not be bounced around which keeps it from cracking or being damaged. When applied to humans it means you are offering enough to keep them warm but not enough to make them deal with whatever they should be dealing with. For the most part your keeping them comfortable and at ease so they will not try to move out of their safe haven. The water never gets hot enough for them to become independent. Because they never have to face the hard facts or situations they never develop the ability to work through things. Their wisdom never develops so they will never understand what to avoid or what is best for them. They will always turn to you for answers instead of developing a relationship with God and finding the best way through all things.

As I write this my nephew again comes to mind. He thought he was not a mercy person because he would not coddle, yet his life is full of mercy for others. A similar thought comes about my sister. She once said to me, "I am not compassionate." but she's the first person I call when my emotions are our of control. She has the compassion to listen to me and let me know it's not weird or unusual to experience those feelings, but she will not coddle me, for which I am extremely grateful.

You see, their type of mercy and compassion encourages life which requires growth. Coddling stifles life and encourages dependency. Mercy and compassion lead people to strength and hope. Coddling leads to frailty and despair.

Encouragement

As Christians one of our greatest and most fulfilling, assignments is to encourage those around us. Encouragement is one of the best ways to express Christ within us. It is, in our world, an unusual and much desired characteristic. Those who encourage stand apart.

Encouragement is the act of showing support, approval and giving hope. It is uplifting to others. When we encourage we are helping others see their value and possibilities. Properly used it can remove fear and depression. Improperly it causes dependency and enables people to remain where they are.

Perhaps the best way to understand is to break it down into it's elements. When we speak of support we are not suggesting the extreme. Encouragement does not mean providing for others to the extent they need to do nothing for themselves. Healthy support does occasionally include assisting someone financially or physically. It more often means listening and assisting where possible. For example, someone is trying to overcome a habit or problem. To encourage them with support you could call or visit often, asking them how they are progressing. If they are having difficulty support them by helping them stay focused or showing them the progress they have made already. You could also let them know you are available to listen whenever they need a genuinely concerned ear. Encouraging support means to do what you can to assist them toward their goal without doing it for them. It requires a great deal of wisdom to recognize when to do for and when to lift up. Learning to ask the Holy Spirit for direction is an invaluable tool when you desire to support others.

Approval is another part of encouragement. This does not mean dishonest approval, or telling someone you approve when they are obviously doing something wrong. For example, it is not appropriate to approve of someone's behavior if the path they are on is self destructive. Appropriate approval comes into play when we see someone is trying to change bad behavior or establish a worthwhile goal in their lives. We can let them know we see value in their actions and direction. This, of coarse, needs to be done without condescending behavior. Sometimes all it takes is letting them know you think it is a good idea or a good goal.

Hope is something we all need at one time or another. Discouraged people often can only see the immediate surroundings or the next step. Often it seems as if a dark and unassailable wall exists before them. Hope lifts their eyes past the immediate and directs them toward a distant light. Like plants, people grow toward light. Offering the hope of light coming can change a persons demeanor and infuse them with the needed strength to stay in the right direction and take the next step. Problems and pathways are not endless. People need to be given the hope that they can not only survive but thrive and grow as they move forward.

Encouragement also means helping people see the valuable parts of their lives. So often people have their faults and mistakes pointed out to them. We should always try to emphasis the good in them. It has been documented that when a person is given a real compliment and encouraged in something they are good at, they often will begin to change those things that are negative. People need to know there are positives in them so they can use those things to build upon. By encouraging them in the good they do, or in the things they do well we are helping them build a foundation that will withstand hard times and give them hope. We can grow more seeds with sweet water than with salt water. We can help people grow in their lives with the sweet water of encouragement rather than the salt water of criticism.

Patience

Patience, the characteristic we recognize as so important and the one we tend to lose more easily than our car keys. Personally, I would recommend you not pray for patience but let God develop it in you along with trust and faith. God will always be faithful to answer your prayer but a crash coarse on patience can be very difficult on you and your family.

Patience is a by product of trust and faith. Like the best cheese and wine its quality improves over time as you walk through life. It begins as we recognize how God works out problems in our daily lives. It becomes part of our character as we realize that few things require immediate solutions or instant results. It is a spiritual fruit that, like all fruit, requires attention and occasional pruning.

Patience is the ability to pass through difficulties and periods of waiting in a calm, self-controlled manner. It is an act of will in that you are willing to tolerate delays while displaying healthy behavior. Patient people do not express willingness to wait then begin to fidget, snap at others or pace. They do not demand instant gratification, but are content to look to the future and wait for greater rewards.

Picture a gardener. He carefully tills the soil and ensures the conditions are right to produce the healthiest plants. He plants the seeds then goes to bed. He does not wake up the next morning expecting fully mature plants with ripe fruit. He does not become angry and rant because the first leaves have not appeared over night. He does not start digging up the seeds to see of the root has begun to develop.

The gardener knows and accepts it will take time for moisture and sunlight to energize the seeds for growth. Fully mature plants will develop but not until the smaller seedling stage is past. Fruit will appear and ripen but not until the flower has bloomed and been pollinated. This acceptance and knowledge of the natural coarse of events gives the gardener patience to wait for the end product while he continues with the endless tasks of weeding, watering, and fertilizing. Diligence and patience are rewarded when the fruit is at the perfect ripeness.

Patience is an active choice that becomes easier the more it is used. It also seems to be easier to be patient when it is recognized as a choice and not a restriction. One rails against restrictions but accepts choices. By recognizing patience as a choice you can move smoothly into waiting while continuing your diligence. Remember the gardener. His patience, or season of waiting, did not mean inactivity. Even patient people have work to do while they wait. Although the event you wait for can not be forced to maturity, you have responsibilities to maintain.

Perhaps one of the greatest benefits of patience and waiting is the opportunity it provides to pull some weeds and loosen some dirt so light and water can get in. There is also time to fertilize with the food of God's word and His presence so the fruit can be enjoyed to the fullest.

Longsuffering

Sounds hard and painful doesn't it. Yet, there is more to longsuffering than gritting your teeth and trying to outlast the situations or circumstances. To truly fit into the scheme of Godly life, it needs to be recognized as an attitude, a response.

I particularly like the definition of makrothumeo (pronounced mak-roth-oo-mee-o), the Greek word translated as longsuffering in the New Testament.

1. To be of a long spirit, not to lose heart
2. To be mild and slow to avenge
3. Slow to anger, slow to punish

It becomes clearest to me when I think of longsuffering as long in spirit. The more time spent with God, the longer your spirit becomes as you reach more and more for God. You are less likely to be offended, thrown off coarse or troubled by circumstances. As your spirit lengthens you see things from a more elevated perspective so you are capable of responding to life with patience and endurance rather than reacting from fear, anger or the need to be justified. Longsuffering is the ability to stand firm in the face of hurricane force winds because your spirit is anchored above the storm, in God.

forbearance

As longsuffering requires patience, forbearance requires self-control. It is the active choice not to retaliate or enforce some debt or obligation. As life happens there will be times people will say or do things that injure or affect us. The natural side of our being wants to react to these times by demanding an accounting or repayment. Better known as the eye-for-an-eye judgment.

God, however, directs us to show forbearance during these times. Actually, we rarely need to demand payment or retaliate. God is fully aware of all circumstances in our lives. He is the champion of His children and will handle the problem as long as we are willing to follow His lead and maintain our self control. His solutions are always the best but we need to allow Him to work by having the self-control to step back and not take things into our own hands.

This does not mean that you are a doormat or that you are not suppose to require repayment of debts. We have an obligation to hold people accountable for their monetary debts unless otherwise directed by God. The difference is in the motive. Retaliation is grounded in anger with the intent to make someone pay for a perceived injury. Forbearance is grounded in the love and trust of God and chooses self-control over anger and forgiveness over retaliation.

Review

The previous words are often confused because they intertwine in action as well as occasionally in definition. To help keep them separated I've included a list of short, very basic definitions below. Deeper understanding should be your goal through your developing relationship with God.

Humble-willingness to bend your knee
Gentleness-tender in heart, spirit and touch
Meekness-displaying patience, humility and gentleness
Mercy-choosing to show compassion and favor over judgment
Compassion-understanding others feelings
Patience-calm ability to tolerate delay
Longsuffering-patient endurance, long in spirit
Forbearance-self restraint, not retaliating

I would like to add a word of caution here. Human beings have a tendency to carry things to extremes. God's desire is for balance in our lives. As you spend time with God, ask Him to reveal to you those areas that have gotten out of balance. For example, it is extremely easy to move from compassion to coddling if you get out of perspective. It is easy to take meekness so far to the extreme that you cease to be looked at seriously and your witness for God is negated. In all things seek God's balance. His scales are always perfect.

One can be merciful yet bold, show compassion yet not enable, be gentle yet direct and be meek without being walked over. As Peter said:

> *So don't lose a minute building on what you've been given complementing your basic faith with good character, spiritual understanding, alert discipline, passionate patience, reverent wonder, warm friendliness, and generous love, each dimension fitting into and developing the others.*
> (2Peter 1:5-8 Message)

The more you develop your relationship with Jesus, the Holy Spirit and the Father, the greater their light will shine through you. After all, the only way to develop a good friendship is to spend time with the friend. Your friendship with God will be the most rewarding and will last for all eternity.

Submission

Submissions is not the same as subservience. The submissive person is neither of less value nor are they a slave. Submission has been misused, maligned and abused so often it has become an insult. God, however, never intended for submission to be used as a weapon or excuse to abuse.

Submission is an act of will. It is not something specifically for women but applies equally to men. In its truest form it is the choice to defer to leadership and authority. It has nothing to do with a person's value nor does it imply some weakness of character. Submissive people recognize they are under another person in the chain of command. They also understand the value of remaining under that covering.

Some false concepts attached to submission include loss of self identity, never saying what you think, never doing what you want, and being cowed and browbeaten. All of these concepts come from the misuse and misunderstanding of both submission and authority. The goal of these concepts is to create absolute control over another. The goal of submission is to maintain a safe life structure to live in.

Lets address loss of self identity. Submission works only if the individual maintains their self identity. The truth is, each of us is a unique blend of characteristics and talents. If each of us were a jigsaw puzzle piece we would have a very specific spot in the puzzle. Our self identity is the unique shape and color for that piece. Without self identity the piece would be blank, leaving a gap in the picture. If your going to fit where you belong you need to maintain your identity so you can fulfill the purpose you were designed for.

God also expects that you will say what you think. Although you are under an authority, they are not God, so you may have some information or idea they need. Remember though, just because you've stated your opinion or idea it does not require your authority to use it. Part of submission is recognizing your authority has to weigh many factors into a decision. Sometimes your idea fits, sometimes it doesn't. It is not a statement about your value. It is about things including you but not exclusive to you.

Submission does require the strength of character to support the one in authority over you. This does not mean doing anything they ask especially if it is illegal or morally wrong. It does mean you behave in a manner that supports that decision. Submission recognizes that authority is there for their protection and will help work to maintain that protection.

Authority

A person in authority, as God intended it, will need humility, patience, longsuffering, forbearance—well pretty much everything examined to this point. Ultimately authority means you get to make the rules and have the final say. The type of authority, the type of leader, you are will be determined by what controls your heart.

The authority figure whose world is small (the size of self) will make decisions based upon themselves and what is convenient for them. Authority figures with a world large enough to encompass the needs of others, an overall plan and directions and a long term goal or vision will make decisions based upon the good of those over whom they have authority.

Those who have a good grasp on the concept of authority recognize that God has given them resources in the people under them. They are fully aware that the people they lead may have a clearer idea of how to make their job more efficient or how to deal with a problem.

A good leader is also concerned with the growth and development of those under them. They will encourage that growth, yet also stay on the alert for things that will cause problems and/or injury. They will be able to make the decision to end something because they have the wisdom to see where damage will occur.

God, the ultimate authority, is weaving individual into amazing artistry using their varied talents and abilities. Human authority should follow that example and weave strength, character, encouragement and purpose into his authority.

Influence

How often we talk about influencing our community and family for Christ. It sounds very benign and "Christ-like." The problem is when you don't understand or know how to influence you can crate some very adverse reactions and situations. The "influence" of many Christians actually drives people from God. It is extremely hard to overcome some well-meaning, uninformed individual's attempt to influence others.

Let's start with what influence is not. It is not manipulation. It is not browbeating or attempting to overpower with words or pamphlets. It is not using condemnation to corner them until they feel there is no escape except to say what you want to hear.

Influence is derived from the Latin word influx which means to flow in. When you influence someone your actions or words flow into their lives. Notice this is flow not flood. There is no force exerted when influencing another. It is a flowing or gentle introduction, usually unnoticed at first. The affect seems to be associated with you but there appears to be no direct effort on your part. In other words, influence is a result of your words and actions as you go about the business of life.

Does this mean you do things specifically designed to produce an effect? That can be calculated manipulation and, since it is a lie will crumble eventually. It crumbles because the only reason you are doing something is to create a specific result. When the result is achieved you stop, revealing the manipulation and creating a problem. The person you are manipulating will often reject what is good for them because the pain from being manipulated will be associated with what you were trying to produce.

For example, you desire to lead someone to Christ. You start a campaign designed to "influence" their decision and change your actions around them to accomplish your goal. It is not about their salvation. It is about you leading them to Christ. "Look God, another trophy for you." After your goal is accomplished you change your behavior, leaving them confused and abandoned.

The only way to truly influence anyone is to live your life as God intended. Be honest and open, yet do not overpower them with scripture and lengthy lectures. Let the light in you become the spark in their darkness by simply being the child of God you are.

In my own life I have been amazed at the way simply doing what God wants and expects from me has opened doors. Through my recent difficulties I determined to do my work as if God was writing my paycheck. That meant being consistent, honest, considerate and conscientious even when I wanted to throw my hands in the air and quit. Frankly I had no heart or energy to actively pursue discussing salvation with anyone but I was honest about my beliefs and church associations. Interestingly enough, by doing it God's way and allowing my life to flow into those around me the opportunity has presented itself often. It has not been forced, staged or calculated. Conversations have naturally flowed that way. I have no "trophies" in that no one has accepted Jesus with me, but there are seeds out there being nurtured by God.

I have determined to flow rather than flood because a flood washes away seeds and my only "trophy" would then be a barren landscape.

Witness

Hand in hand with influence comes witness. As with most English words it has a variety of meanings. Witness comes from the Old English word wit which means knowledge. The American Heritage Dictionary lists many meanings, however, the most basic is-something that serves as a sign.

This definitions seems to express the best concept of a witness for Christ. As Witnesses we serve as signs for a lost world. In a sense, to be a witness means you are a sign post directing others to God and enabling them to enjoy the privileges of adoption.

We are all aware of the verbal witness. Someone talks to another about Christ and His redemptions. This is the final step in witnessing, not the first or only step. The most influential witness is the one whose life is a witness, or sign post. This requires diligence, understanding, mercy,compassion and a progressively closer walk with God. As you go through life you live it honestly and transparently. You can't be an effective witness if you portray yourself as always happy and unmoved by life. It is not reality and tends to make you unapproachable. Reality is good and bad times; sadness and elation; and closeness as well as distance. Effective witnesses are those who let people know about the tough times. Contrary to popular belief it is how we act in the tough times that witnesses to more people. They see you getting through with hope and vitality rather than despair and depression. Your hope in bad times opens more doors than hiding what you are going through.

In my own life I have had more opportunity to talk about Jesus when I am in or getting out of a hard time. Every time someone has seen things turn around they comment on how lucky I am. What more perfect time to tell them about God's love, grace and power? As a matter of interest I have also noticed it is not the see-through, cracked human side of me they remember but the individual that trusted God. The hope and vitality that remained even when the human was bone weary and miserable.

Perhaps witnessing is more about the seeds we plant as we walk through the fields of life.

Commitment

Somehow, over time, commitment and covenant have become synonymous. Although they are similar, there are some very basic and important differences between them.

To commit is to pledge to do something or meet a requirement. For example, parents commit to spending one evening a week with their children in quality time. We commit to our jobs, agreeing to be there on time and follow through with our work. We commit to help in some church function or ministry.

In each of these cases we choose to perform some action for a limited time. Commitments are negotiable and will vary over time and circumstances. Our children grow and establish their own homes so our pledge to spend one night per week with them becomes null. We may remain in the same job for years but eventually we will end that commitment by either moving to another job or retiring. Church functions last only a short time and God may move us into another ministry.

Commitments are an essential part of life. Holding to a commitment develops character in our lives. We learn diligence and perseverance as well as establishing a foundation of trust with those around us. Making and keeping commitments help to establish unity in our lives.

Covenant

A covenant is a pledge established between two people which states specific conditions required by both parties as well as consequences should the covenant be broken. The covenant is considered binding until death and can be considered eternal, to be honored by following generations. Unlike a commitment, covenants have a distinct spiritual element to them.

The Old Testament Hebrew word berith is translated as covenant. It is derived from a root word that mean "to cut." During that era of history a covenant was established by cutting an animal in half and walking between the halves. The significance of this becomes clearer when we remember that taking a life, even of an animal unless it was for food, was a serious event. I look at it this way, the one thing a human can not give back once it's taken is life. To establish an agreement that requires the ending of a life shows the seriousness of that agreement. Let me state this another way. You can not restart life after it has been ended. An agreement that requires the ending of a life is binding until that life can be restarted, which can not happen if the animal is cut in half. Although covenants no longer require this sacrifice, they are no less binding.

As an example, the original covenant between God and Adam was established by God wherein God promised life, protection and fellowship with Adam who was responsible for his domain given only one condition, to not eat from the trees of live and knowledge. The promise was life the penalty was death.

Adam broke the covenant thereby bringing death and separation from God into man's existence. Although the penalty had to be enacted, God loves so much He devised a plan to restore the original covenant. He established a sequence of events through out time to bring every condition and circumstance to one point. That point being the moment Jesus died on the cross, assumed the obligation for all mankind, suffered the penalty for us and allowing us the choice to enter into the original covenant with god. In effect god renewed the original covenant by making an eternal agreement with Himself, God incarnate in Jesus, whereby Jesus took our penalty and satisfied the conditions of the covenant. No other man could establish that agreement. It now only requires you choose to move into the eternal covenant.

Worship

We were designed to worship which should be an encouragement to us. Unfortunately our lack of understanding often prevents us from enjoying the benefits. For some people "worship" has become encrusted with so many repugnant ideas it repels them from God.

The Hebrew word for worship is derived from the same word as humble. If we have a poor understanding of humility, our ability to worship will be impaired. The reverse is also true. If our concept of worship implies demeaning, degrading or demoralizing behavior, we will have trouble understanding humility.

As I discussed under humble, the root word means to bend your knee. Understand there is no implication of force applied to make you bend your knee. It is an act of free will. You choose to bend your knee not from the stand, "You should be honored that I bow to you." But from the realistic stand that there is something greater than yourself.

Worship can be expressed in many different ways. Singing praises is usually the first idea that comes to mind. God has put in us an interesting trait. When we sing or hear music our soul tends to open and become more accessible to God. Musical worship is a very powerful tool.

Worship also includes standing before God and expressing

your wonder and awe of His greatness. It does not matter how you say it. He only desires that you tell Him from your heart. The most elaborate and wordy praises mean nothing if they are simply repeated renditions. To truly worship you need to tell Him what you see in Him that sparks your adoration and moves your spirit. I truly believe that telling God He does amazing things with clouds and colors is as much worship as a long chant listing His attributes.

We also worship God when we choose to be obedient to His leading. As we develop our relationship with God we become more aware of His voice. As we read His word we become more aware of how He expects us to live our lives. Following His lead and being obedient to His call is an act of worship. We are bending our knee in acknowledgement of His greatness and wisdom.

One point is very important to clarify here. Worship is not an ego trip for God. Unlike people who desire to be worshipped to boost their selfish ego, God does not need us to worship Him in order for Him to be God. God is complete whether you worship Him or not. He does not need to be "fluffed" or inflated. He has been, is now, and will always be exactly like He is regardless of our actions.

As with all things God asks of us, worship is for our benefit. When we worship we open the lines of communication between ourselves and God. Our worship allows Him into the place He most desires, as close to us as possible. During this time He is given the opportunity to help us by revelation, healing and the impartation of wisdom. God wishes you to worship so the door to an abundant life can be opened. Bending your knee is a small act which leads to God sized treasure.

$\mathcal{G}$*race*

Grace is one of those words that can be extremely confusing to people raised outside of the church. It is usually only used in reference to a prayer before special meals or to describe the beauty and flow of a persons movements. After accepting Jesus as Lord I began to hear of God's grace. I realized it meant something different than I was used to but the meaning seemed vague.

Grace was usually express as the free, unearned gift of God. That's nice. Free is good. What exactly was I receiving? Salvation. Yes, I could understand that but there seemed to be the implication of something deeper, bigger, more profound. There in lies the trap that can lead people to mysticism and cults. Definitions can be just that simple, and equally that profound.

Among the many definitions for grace is, a favor rendered by one who need not do so. In the dictionary this definition is listed completely separate from all those pertaining to God and religion. Perhaps it's the clearest for that very reason. It aims straight at the heart of God's grace,.

God did not have to bestow salvation on us. Man broke the covenant with God which resulted in the consequence of death. God could have walked away and washed His hands of man. Instead, He spent millennium working out a precise, complete plan to bring man the opportunity to return. Man could not have done, and still can not do, what would be required to rectify the broken covenant. God rendered us the favor of return to His present and renewal of the covenant at a high price, even though He was not required to do so.

Actually, God does not have to do anything for us. Most of the time we are more like oblivious children than worthy servants. Even the best of us can not be good enough to earn favors from God. He bestows the privilege of adoption on us because He wants to. He honors us with His presence and Holy Spirit because it is His desire to be close to us, not because we are good enough.

Grace, the undeserved favor, the unearned delight of God.

Joy

We all know what joy is, that feeling of elation that comes from everything working out right, being told incredibly good news, or the excitement of seeing your child for the first time. Joy can be an overwhelming emotion, coloring everything you see. Joy can also be so quiet and deep that it is difficult to identify. You actually have to look for it to recognize it.

There is a joy that settles so deep in our souls it remains no matter what adverse conditions are being faced. It is formed by a sense of security that calms us and produces peace deep within us. Like the deep calm of a mountain lake, it lies hidden, breaking to the surface suddenly in sparkling, glittering streams. When it breaks out it reflects the most perfect light in a kaleidoscope of glittering diamonds. It's source is God.

We don't take advantage of this joy as often as we should. When we first accept Jesus it is tangible and exciting, so close to the surface it is visible. Over time it works deeper into our hearts and souls, becoming less obvious although it actually strengthens with the Holy Spirit's care and nurturing. The cares of life can tend to overshadow this joy much like a cloud can overshadow a lake or stream, giving the illusion that the sparkle of light is gone.

You can renew your connection to that joy by renewing your

connection to the source. By working on an interactive relationship with God you can renew the sparkle of your joy and bring it out to the surface again. By interactive I am referring to a well developed, two way communication system between you and God. This requires you set aside your God honey-do list and any formulas you have developed. You will need to learn to actually interact with God, not just petition Him. Conversation requires talk, listen, talk, listen and talk. We need to learn how to actually listen to God in our lives so we can respond to Him as our Father and Friend, not just the man with all the toys.

This is the type of communication that draws that joy to the surface. By talking to God throughout the day, not just during our "prayer" or "quiet" time, we connect to the source of security and allow the joy to sparkle despite the cloud cover because there is no cloud between us and our light.

Look around you during the day and ask God to reveal His wonder and beauty. Become aware and responsive. Let Him color your world with the joy of His love for you. When those clouds do come in, you discover it is easier to find the deep joy that will get you through.

Joy, the elation of peace.

Holy

We use the term holy to describe God without clearly understanding the significance and importance of holiness. For non-Christians holiness is seen as pertaining to objects and God invoking images of extreme consequences if touched or disturbed. It means unapproachable and untouchable with a hint of magic or unfathomable power.

As a child I remember believing that putting anything on top of a Holy Bible would incur God's wrath. I wasn't sure what it meant but I knew I would be in big trouble. Writing or underlining in a Bible would get you sent straight to hell. I have talked to many people with similar concepts. Some believe whatever is holy is beyond their comprehension so they could not understand the bible anyway. Some see holiness as condemning, so they could never approach God. Some see holiness as some very secret, hidden thing that must not be disturbed.

After I accepted Jesus I learned many of my early concepts were false and I could approach God. Writing in a Bible would not damn me. There was still that unclear, half formed understanding that made me feel God's holiness kept me at arms length from Him. I could hear Him, feel His presence but because He was Holy I could not be close to Him. Eventually God broke through those barriers. I discovered holiness had nothing to do with some moral superiority I had to achieve first. It wasn't associated with my value as a human verses God's holiness.

Holy, in reference to people, means we are set aside for God. In the most basic sense it means He has put His stamp of ownership on us. As we progress we learn what He is like and what He desires us to be. This brings us closer to Him and reinforces our holiness, bringing more light to our lives. We become set aside not only in adoption but also in behavior and thinking. The light penetrates us and gives us new perspective on our actions and words making us clearer and more light filled.

God's holiness is complete. There is nothing even remotely like God. He is set aside as Himself. There is no darkness in Him so His light is pure. Since there are spots and corners in humans that are dark, we can not be directly exposed to God's holiness without being destroyed by the revelation of Him versus us. He loves us so much He works with us to expose and remove those dark places slowly and with gentleness so we can be closer to Him.

We need to realize that being holy does not give us a superior standing in the world. It means that we need to act as if we are always alongside God and He is sharing every experience with us. This sets us aside because we avoid those things that God does not like. It does not mean we can't interact with people, enjoy movies and joke around. It means we have a responsibility to do these things in the light because we are set apart for the light.

To maintain your personal holiness you need to stay close to God. His Holiness helps us identify what is darkness and what we should avoid. Staying close to Him helps us avoid the traps of legalism since we align our light with God's and not some set of self-imposed and rigid set of human rules.

It's similar to getting used to certain temperatures in your environment. Your spending a great deal of time outside in, say

45-50 degree weather. Your body adjusts to this temperature. It feels normal to you just as being outside of God feels normal. If you are invited inside where the temperature is perhaps 75, you will be uncomfortable. You will have to change to lighter clothing and adjust your behavior. Over time the 75 degrees becomes normal. It is comfortable and you discover there are many benefits to the warmth. Being in the warmth is like being set aside for God, it's uncomfortable at first but has many new and better benefits.

If you were to go back outside you would discover that what was once normal was now uncomfortable. You would miss the warmth, light and security of being inside. The walls set you aside in safety, warmth and security just as God's holiness sets you aside for all that He is, your security, strength, purpose, hope and wisdom.

Holy-living inside God's warmth and protection, set aside from the cold of separation.

Peace

Peace, the absence of war, a fairly amazing gift if you think about it. Unlike the world's view of peace, the lack of conflict between two armed groups, God's peace deals with the spiritual as well as the personal.

For a moment, lets examine war. It is conflict between two opposing forces. There exists a desire to win or force the opponent to accept and integrate ideals, methods, thought processes and behavior patterns. Wars require one winner and one loser unless a truce is formed which requires an agreement with conditions.

War can be waged within ourselves. Our emotions can war with our intellect. Our spiritual man can war with our natural man. These conflicts are most readily recognized by the confusions and opposing actions in our lives. Our emotions want us to react to our environment, retaliating, clinging or crying our way out of situations. Our intellect believes we can reason our way out and that everyone can be rational at all times. Our natural man wants to linger in the realm of instant gratification and satisfy our emotions, no matter how temporary. Our spiritual man wants to linger close to God, satisfying our hunger for light. Most often, if left unresolved these conflicts result in condemnation, stubbornness, depression and anger.

When Jesus said He had come to give us peace, not as the world knows it but godly peace, He was referring to the inner turmoil of man. He was saying there would always be conflicts from outside we will have to deal with, but, those inner conflicts that inhibit our ability to handle outside circumstances will be resolved. Put more simply, your battles will be fought on one front, not two.

How does this work, this peace that passes all understanding? It is the calm that develops from knowing you are loved, completely, unconditionally and with great delight. You don't have to earn this love, just accept it. It is not contingent upon your doing the right sequence of steps in prayer or daily life. You are loved because you were created to be loved by God. This is perhaps the hardest truth for many to accept, especially if we have been rejected or abused by people, but it is true. I encourage you to spend time with God and ask Him to make this reality for you. You will be amazed at the peace you will have.

This is important for many reasons. Knowing this truth beyond question develops an inner contentment that dampens our reactions and holds our emotions and desires in a binding truce with our minds and spirits. It is not a absence of emotion but the removal of emotions as controls in our lives. Our emotions begin to align with the Spirit of God. Rather than overpowering us our emotions become tools in line with our spirit giving us purpose and strength.

This lack of war within ourselves reduces anxiety and stress. It opens the curtains in our lives to allow the light both in from God and out to people. Knowing you are safe in God helps you face the turmoil of life with an inexplicable calm. It is like being in the eye of a hurricane. All around you are the winds of destruction but you are standing in peace.

The peace of God is like a mountain lake, so tranquil, so deep the hidden lights within us can shine forth.

Glory

As a new Christian I was confused by the expression "Give God the Glory." It seemed to me that God already had all the glory since He was God. I also began to realize that I didn't understand what glory really meant.

Scanning through the Hebrew I discovered the words used to describe God's glory meant:

To be heavy, to be made heavy, enjoy honor, be weighty, make oneself

dense, numerous, cloak-holy adornment, valuable, prized, eminence,

endurance in time

God's glory is the dense weight of His holy cloak, existing through all time, filled with honor and prestige. It is real and tangible. Its weight displaces everything else leaving room only for God. There is no beginning or end to it, nor does it fade.

The immensity of God's glory was experienced by the Israelites when they completed the temple Solomon built and dedicated to God. God, Himself, sanctified the temple, filling it with His glory, His cloak of authority and honor. The people had to leave the temple because it was so dense. Its brightness was intolerable to human eyes.

Although being exposed to God's complete glory would crush

us, He does allow us glimpses of its magnificent. Sometimes it is the tangible weight from outside ourselves as we worship and pray. Sometimes it's the spiritual reaction to His presence as we move close to Him. Sometimes it's the actual light of His glory we see.

Shortly after I accepted Jesus I was blessed to experience His glory first hand. I worked as an X-ray tech and on one particularly busy day I went to lunch late. The cafeteria was not full so I chose a table in the corner where I could read the Bible undisturbed. Suddenly I became aware that the Bible, table, even the air around me seemed denser and more brightly lit than normal. The cafeteria had no windows so it wasn't the sun coming from behind a cloud. The lights had all been on so it wasn't a change in lighting. When I looked up I realized every other person and object seemed to be darker, less real than the area I sat in. Later, God often brought that experience to mind to help me endure. I knew His glory never faded although the light was not visible to my natural eye.

Giving God the Glory, the term that confused me so as a young Christian, does not mean that we pass the mantle of glory to God. It means that we acknowledge His possession and direct the honor for His work to the source, God. We can not accept the weight of His glory or the praise that rightly belongs to Him.

Anointed

The Christian culture uses the word anointed almost as often as God. We speak of being anointed, anointing the sick and the anointing of God. To those raised outside the church the meaning of those phrases can be easily understood, and just as easily misunderstood.

Anointing means to spread on or pour on oil, to take away ashes. What can pouring or spreading oil on something have to do with God and how does it fit with being anointed? We use oil at the beach to protect our skin and enhance our tan. Dry hair is given an oil treatment which helps give it back its strength and vitality. Shepherds use oil on sheep to protect them from harmful insect bites (it works on people against mosquitoes too.) Oil when spread on the skin is absorbed into the body. It smoothes and sooths rough skin and aids the skin's ability to protect the body from harmful elements.

The anointing of God works in much the same way. The oil of God's Spirit spreads over us and enhances the talents and gifts God has placed within us, much like the oil treatment enhances your hair. As we absorb God's anointing it protects us from the harmful bites of temptation and attack like oil at the beach protects us from sunburn. Our spiritual skin is smoothed and soothed so its beauty can shine as a beacon to those around us.

Anointing or putting oil on the sick is a symbol of removing the ashes from the sick. It is designed to give us a focal point from which we receive God's promise of healing. The oil itself is not the agent. The Spirit of God and the power of God are the source. It is the acceptance and absorption of God's promise that brings healing.

Conviction vs. Condemnation

I'm electing to cover these two words together because they are often considered to have the same meaning or their meanings are reversed. The non-Christian cultures especially have a misconception concerning these two words that actually drive people away from God. Unfortunately legalism in the church has helped to reinforce the misconceptions.

Conviction is an adjective derived from the word convince. It means that one believes something to be true. When a jury convicts a felon of a crime they are expressing their belief that the evidence is true and the felon did what he is accused of. Within the realm of the Christian culture we speak of being convicted by God. It is a slightly misleading phrase since God is not convinced by the evidence and standing as a jury over us. We are the ones who are being convinced by the evidence. The reality is that God is shining His light into an area of our lives revealing evidence to our spirit. We become convicted because we believe the evidence he shows us is true. Instead of saying "God has convicted us," it would be much more accurate to say "God has shown me a truth about something in my life and I am convinced He is right." Being convinced He is right gives us the opportunity to regret the separation it creates between us, apologize for that separation and move to correct it. There is a certain amount of pain associated with this process because humans really hate being shown both their mistakes and their inappropriate behavior. Recognizing the pain for what it is (the pain of separation) and using it to return to God is referred to as repentance.

Condemnation, on the other hand, is not about being convinced of some truth. It is about being disapproved of. Instead of light it carries with it the darkness of guilt and a sense of unworthiness. Condemnation brings with it a desire to run and hide in shame. We are likely to continue in our wrong behavior rather than turn from it because condemnation does not offer a way out, or rather up. Condemnation's path is downward.

The Abundant Life

Through out this book, and in the Christian culture, we talk about having life more abundantly or the abundant life. God's intention was for us to live an abundant life in Eden. Jesus died to give us the opportunity to move into abundant life now. For some this generates visions of life without problems or concerns. For others, a life of wealth and prosperity is imagined. Others see abundant life as extremely active. Each conceives of an idealistic life, a concept that opens the door for discouragement and burnout. Often, because things do not fit with their concept of abundant life, people become depressed and pick up unwarranted condemnation.

The first thing we need to understand is life. The American Heritage Dictionary defines life as:

1. The physical, mental, and spiritual experiences that constitute existence

2. Human existence, relationships or activities in general

3. A source of vitality, animating force.

Life is that force that enables you to move through time, interacting with others through relationships, your environment, and God.

Abundance means to be full, rich and plentiful. Anything that exists in large quantities is said to be abundant.

If we unite the two meanings we discover that abundant life is not about what you acquire or gain in the physical sense. Abundant life means you have a plentiful, rich and full source of vitality and animation. Or, put another way, the vitality of your life is a quality source energizing you to move.

Consider the person with a good job and family who works everyday, comes home, spends evenings enjoying family and friends, goes to bed and wakes up the next morning to repeat this process yet the meaning behind all these things is intangible. They do it because they are suppose to, probably even enjoy much of it. Somehow, despite all the activity there is the nagging question, "Is this all?"

Sadly this can be the Christian as well. The activity level of Christians can be unbelievably busy because they include church and ministries with everyday life. Although they have filled the "God shaped" space in their lives, they have not, necessarily filled the abundant life gap. Sometimes it's because they don't understand abundant life. Sometimes it's because they misunderstand many of the words we have discussed here. This person is trying to mold themselves into definitions either handed to them or developed by themselves. Rather than produce a fully vital and animated life, their misconceptions tie them with false ideas and invisible ropes. Instead of joy, the awe of God's glory and peace, they labor under heavy rocks. How can you experience joy if the rock you carry says to be humble you must recognize you are worthless? You can't have abundant life if you believe God sees no value in you. How can your life be animated if you believe meekness turns you into some kind of subhuman? You can't revel in the glory of God's friendship if you believe to be submissive you must cease to be who God created you to be.

Abundant life means you are passing through time and space, developing a relationship with God and tapping into the infinite source of vitality and animation. This doesn't mean you won't be tired, annoyed, frustrated or discouraged at times. What it means is that life, itself, becomes more real. Instead of an endurance test it becomes an experience. Instead of dry, God fills your life with oasis's and rivers. Instead of lacking color you marvel at the rainbows in everyday life. Your not euphoric or "high" but aware, alert, capable, stronger and more confident because, no matter what, there is a gentle, loving, overflowing source that leads and helps you. Above all that infinite source desires to move through time and space holding your hand.

Dear God,
Let the knowledge presented here lead to understanding, understanding to wisdom, and wisdom to continuous flow of vitality and animation from Your infinite source for all those who read these words.

I came that they may have and enjoy life, and have it in abundance.
John 10:10 (Amplified)

Appendix

Printed in the United States
150485LV00002B/90/A

9 781424 112289